AnimalWays

Bats

AnimalWays

Bats

SUE RUFF AND DON E. WILSON

BENCHMARK BOOKS

MARSHALL CAVENDISH
NEW YORK

With thanks to Dr. Dan Wharton,
director of the Central Park Wildlife Center,
for his expert reading of this manuscript.

Benchmark Books
Marshall Cavendish Corporation
99 White Plains Road
Tarrytown, NY 10591-9001

Library of Congress Cataloging-in-Publication Data
Ruff, Sue.
Bats / by Sue Ruff and Don E. Wilson.
p. cm. — (Animalways)
Includes bibliographical references (p.   ).
Summary: Provides information on the physical characteristics, behavior, habitat, and
various species of bats.
ISBN 0-7614-1137-2
1. Bats—Juvenile literature. [1. Bats.] I. Wilson, Don E. II. Title. III. Animal ways
(Tarrytown, N.Y.)
QL737.C5 R83   2001   599.4—dc21   99-058684

Photo research by Candlepants, Inc.

Cover photo: Animals Animals/Oxford Scientific Films

The photographs in this book are used by permission and through the courtesy of: *Photo
Researchers, Inc.*: Merlin C. Tuttle/Bat Conservation International, 2, 53, 66, 70, 71, 73, 76;
Larry Miller, 37 (lower); William Ervin/Science Photo Library, 47; Jonathon Watts, 56 (top);
Stephon Dalton, 69, back cover; Virginia Weinland, 82. *Animals Animals:* Micheal FogDen,
9, 37 (center); Hans & Judy Beste,13; John Gerlach, 17, 63 (inset); Ken G. Preston-
Mafham, 21; ES/ER/Degghiger, 25; B & B Wells, Oxford Science Films, 36 (top); Richard
LaVal, 37 (top), 79; Joe McDonald, 41, 65; Bruce Davidson, 44; Stephen Dalton/Oxford
Science Films, 56 (low), 57; J. Brown/Oxford Science Films, 60; Paul Freed, 63; Klaus
Uhlenhut, 75. *Bat Conservation International:* Merlin C. Tuttle,15, 18, 32, 36 (lower), 51, 85,
87. Steve Walker, 89.

Printed in Italy

6 5 4 3 2 1

Contents

Animal Kingdom

CNIDARIANS

coral

ARTHROPODS
(animals with
jointed limbs and
external skeleton)

MOLLUSKS

squid

CRUSTACEANS

crab

ARACHNIDS

spider

INSECTS

grasshopper

MYRIAPODS

centipede

CARNIVORES

lion

SEA MAMMALS

whale

PRIMATES

orangutan

HERBIVORES
(5 orders)

elephant

PHYLA

ANNELIDS

earthworm

CHORDATES
(animals with a dorsal nerve chord)

ECHINODERMS

starfish

SUB PHYLA

VERTEBRATES
(animals with a backbone)

CLASSES

FISH   **BIRDS**   **MAMMALS**   **AMPHIBIANS**   **REPTILES**

fish   gull   frog   snake

ORDERS

RODENTS   **INSECTIVORES**   **MARSUPIALS**   **SMALL MAMMALS**
(several orders)

squirrel   mole   koala   **BAT**

1 The World of Bats

As darkness falls, a hungry bat wakes up and stretches its wings. Then it flies from its roost to a nearby cow pasture in search of food. It swoops back and forth over the field until its sensitive ears pick up the gentle sound of a sleeping cow's breathing. The bat lands on the ground near the cow. This is a vampire bat, and the cow's blood will be its dinner.

The bat circles the sleeping cow, searching for a good place to feed. It uses a flap of skin on its nose that acts as a heat detector to find a warm spot where the cow's blood flows close to the skin. The bat quickly finds what it is looking for. It chews away a little patch of hair, exposing the cow's skin. Then it bites the cow and starts to drink its blood. The big animal sleeps unaware.

The cow does not feel the tiny, shallow bite of the bat's razor-sharp teeth. Its blood continues to flow. The bat's saliva contains an anticoagulant—a chemical that keeps the blood from clotting. The bat starts to feed, using its tongue almost like a straw.

VAMPIRE BATS ARE THE ONLY MAMMALS IN THE WORLD THAT LIVE ENTIRELY ON BLOOD.

As soon as it starts to feed, the bat also begins to urinate. Why? Blood is about half water. The bat is getting rid of the water, which it doesn't need and which would make it too heavy to fly. It keeps only the nourishing part of the blood. When the bat has drunk about two tablespoons, it is so full it can hardly fly. It flings itself into the air—most bats can't take off from the ground, but vampire bats can—and flies back to its roost.

At the roost, if another vampire bat has not found food, the full bat will regurgitate a little blood for the empty bat. It might be saving the other bat's life. Vampire bats have to eat at least every two days or they will die.

How big are these bloodsucking monsters? Pick up a little bag of potato chips, one that weighs about 1.5 ounces (43 grams). That's the average weight of a common vampire bat. With its wings folded, a vampire bat could sit easily on the palm of your hand. With its long wings stretched out, it measures about 12 to 14 inches (30–36 cm) from wing tip to wing tip. There are three species of vampire bat. The common vampire lives on the blood of mammals or birds, while evidence points to the other two species' preference for the blood of birds. Vampire bats usually do not bother humans.

Where Are Bats Found?

Have you ever seen a bat up close? Probably not. They are nocturnal, that is, active at night. And they are shy. If you have seen one at all, it probably fluttered past your head when you were out walking, just after sunset. During the day, bats roost in places where you are unlikely to see them: behind the bark of a tree or hanging from the ceiling of a cave or an attic.

There are more than nine hundred species, or kinds, of bats. They live on every continent on Earth except Antarctica.

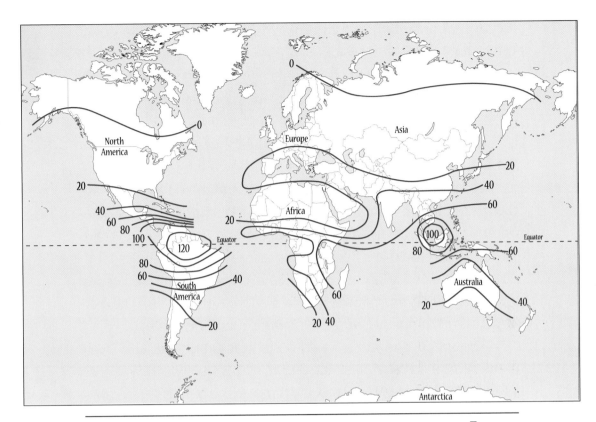

THIS MAP SHOWS THE RICHNESS OF BAT SPECIES THROUGHOUT THE WORLD. THE NUMBER OF BATS INCREASES BY AND LARGE AS THE EQUATOR IS APPROACHED. HOWEVER, FEW BATS LIVE IN THE DESERTS OF THE ARABIAN PENINSULA AND NORTH AFRICA.

Bats are found almost as far north as the Arctic Circle and as far south as Argentina and the southernmost tip of South Africa.

Like all other mammals, bats need food, water, and shelter. Some species—including the three kinds of vampire bats—live in warm climates where food is available all year long. Others migrate or hibernate (or both) when cold weather comes and their food supply disappears. Bats are found in all kinds of habitats: mountains, deserts, forests, and grasslands. Some bats live far from people. Others live on farms, in suburbs, and even in towns and cities.

Tropical Bats. Food is available all year long in tropical rain forests. Most rain-forest bats eat plant foods—fruit, nectar, or pollen. Others prey on insects or larger creatures.

Blossom bats live in Australia and eat nectar and pollen. To feed, a hungry blossom bat lands on a flowering plant. It pokes its nose into a flower and uses its long, brush-tipped tongue to lap the nectar. Pollen from the flower clings to its fur and wings. The bat moves from blossom to blossom, feeding and pollinating the plants. When the bat is full, it flies to a tree and hangs by its hind claws from a roost hidden in the leaves. It grooms itself, licking and swallowing the pollen, its main source of protein. The bat depends on the plants, and the plants depend on the bat.

The spectacled flying fox, a huge fruit-eating bat, also lives in the Australian rain forest. It especially likes fruit with tiny seeds, such as figs. Fig seeds pass quickly through the bat's digestive system. New fig trees sprout where the seeds fall to the ground in its droppings. By spreading the seeds, the bat helps to preserve its habitat.

In an African rain forest, a large slit-faced bat hangs from a tree, listening for movement. When it hears a frog it swoops down, catches it, and flies to a hollow tree to feed. Large slit-faced bats also catch and eat beetles, crickets, small birds, and fish. Sometimes they even prey on smaller bats. There are not many caves in the rain forest, so many species of bats, including the large slit-faced bat, roost in hollow trees.

Short-tailed fruit bats have to be more flexible in their eating habits. They live in tropical wet and dry habitats, where there are three distinct seasons: cool and dry, hot and dry, and hot and wet. The diet of the short-tailed fruit bat is most varied in the dry season, when less ripe fruit is available. In Costa Rica,

FLYING FOXES LIVE IN THE TROPICS WHERE FRUIT, NECTAR, AND POLLEN ARE AVAILABLE YEAR-ROUND.

where scientists have studied them, the bats eat fruit from more than fifty different kinds of plants. They eat nectar and pollen, too, and sometimes insects.

Bats in tropical wet and dry habitats may migrate short distances to find flowering or fruit-bearing plants or a source of water, but they do not have to cope with cold weather and severe food shortages.

Desert Bats. Just north and south of the tropics lie the subtropics. This is where most of the world's deserts are found. Deserts can be sandy or rocky, flat or mountainous. They can be hot, temperate, or cold. Bats live in hot deserts year-round and in temperate deserts for part of the year. They can't live in very cold, or polar, deserts at all.

Pallid bats are summer residents of the temperate deserts of the southwestern United States. They are famous for being able to snatch scorpions from the desert floor without getting stung. They roost in rocky outcrops during the day, coming out at night to hunt for beetles, grasshoppers, moths, scorpions, and even lizards. Not much is known about their winter habits. They probably do not migrate, but may fly deep into caves or mine shafts to hibernate during the cold months. Long-tongued and long-nosed bats live in these deserts, too, but they feed on fruits, pollen, and nectar. These bats have long snouts and tongues that can poke deep into blossoms. They are especially fond of large agave plants and some species of cactus.

When the weather gets cooler and plants stop blooming, long-tongued and long-nosed bats head south to Mexico and Central America, where they can still find food. The bats have to follow a route where they can feed every night. Insect-eating bats that migrate must find nourishment along the way.

Temperate Forest Bats. Forests make great habitats for insect-eating bats. There are several kinds of temperate forests, and bats live in all of them.

Summers are hot and winters are cold in eastern North America, western Europe, and eastern Asia. Here, in temperate deciduous forests, the trees grow new leaves in the spring and shed them in the fall. Bats arrive in these forests in the spring,

AT NIGHT, WHEN SCORPIONS EMERGE FROM THEIR DAYTIME HIDING PLACES, PALLID
BATS ARE READY TO FEAST ON THEM.

and soon after, the females give birth. When the young are ready to fly and hunt for their own food, insects are abundant. In the fall, the bats disappear. Some migrate; others hibernate. They find a cave, mine tunnel, or some other place where they won't freeze. Their body temperature drops, their heartbeat and breathing slows, and they fall into a deep sleep. Though they wake up briefly from time to time, they basically skip winter.

The northwest coast of the United States has mild winters and plenty of rain. Evergreen forests flourish there—and so do bats. Creatures that need water, such as frogs and snails, live here, too. Keen's myotis is one of many bats that roosts in caves and beneath the bark of trees along the northwest coast. It hunts for insects just after dark and just before dawn. Keen's myotis hibernates in winter.

Coastal areas in the southeastern United States are also rainy but winters are mild. Seminole bats roost in Spanish moss on the Gulf and along the Atlantic coast, hanging beneath loose bark, in clumps of foliage, and sometimes in caves. They hunt in the early evening, sometimes flying around streetlights to catch insects. They also forage around trees, over watercourses, and in clearings. They are seen year-round. They may shift slightly to the southern part of their range in winter, but there is no evidence that they migrate.

Far to the north, winters are long and cold, and summers are short and cool. Wolves, moose, and rabbits live here among the evergreens. In the summer, there are plenty of insects for silver-haired bats to eat. They roost alone or with a few other bats in hollow trees or empty woodpecker nests. They forage for small flying insects, especially moths, in the treetops and over ponds and streams.

Hoary bats also range far to the north in summer. The most widespread of all American bats, they live from northern Canada south throughout the United States and Mexico and into Guatemala. They are also found in Hawaii and South America. Hoary bats roost in foliage, hidden from above, where a soaring hawk might spot them, but visible from below. After a short summer stay in Maine or Canada, do they migrate? Probably. One of the most exciting things about bats is how much we humans still have to discover.

Near the Arctic Circle, at the northernmost edge of the boreal forests, lies the tree line, beyond which trees can't grow. The tree line is also the bat line. Farther north, it is too cold and barren for bats.

THIS HOARY BAT IS NOT SNOW-COVERED; THE TIPS OF ITS FUR ARE WHITE. IT AVOIDS WINTER WEATHER BY HIBERNATING OR MIGRATING.

YELLOW-WINGED BATS LIVE IN AFRICAN GRASSLANDS AND FEED ON INSECTS.

Grassland Bats. Some, but not many, species of bats live in grasslands and savannas. Bats have trouble finding good places to roost in grasslands, where there is not enough rain for trees to grow. The American prairie was a vast grassland before most of it was turned into farmland. There are probably more bats living in the Midwest now than there were two hundred years ago because a farm can provide everything a bat needs: buildings to roost in, water, and insects to eat.

Savannas are tropical grasslands that get rain part of the year but have a long dry season. Trees are widely scattered across them. The Serengeti plain, in East Africa, is a vast savanna. Grazing animals such as zebras, giraffes, and wildebeest live here, along with lions and other predators. The yellow-winged bat lives in the Serengeti and in the savannas of central Africa, roosting near rivers and lakes in shrubs and low trees such as the acacia. These trees flower during the dry season, when insects are scarce. The flowers attract insects, and the bats are there to eat them. Yellow-winged bats—the only bats that have greenish fur and yellowish wings—snatch insects from leaves or swoop down to pick them from the ground.

What Do People Think About Bats?

When European explorers of the Americas came upon bats that drank blood, they compared them to human vampires, who were supposed to return from the dead to suck the blood of their victims. They named the real bats after the old European legends.

The Maya, who lived in Mexico and Central America more than one thousand years ago, gave their god of the underworld the head of a vampire bat. Vampire bats are the only mammals in the world that live on blood, and they helped give bats a bad name. But even before vampire bats were discovered, bats were often pictured by European writers as spooky or evil. In Shakespeare's play *Macbeth*, witches stirred "wool of bats" (bat fur) into a brew. William Cartwright, who lived more than 350 years ago, at about the same time as Shakespeare, wrote "Bless this house. . . . Keep it from all evil spirits, Fairies, weasels, bats, and ferrets."

Today we don't think weasels and ferrets are evil. If we think about fairies at all, we think of them as good, not evil. But sometimes we don't know what to think about bats. We associate them with Halloween and ghost stories and devils. Look closely at a picture of a devil. Do its wings look like bat wings? Devils are often pictured with claws on their feet—like bats. Look at a picture of an angel. Angels' wings usually have feathers, like the wings of birds. You won't find claws on the feet of an angel.

The German word for bat, *fledermaus*, means "flying mouse." Americans say someone is "as blind as a bat." What are bats? Are they mice with wings? Are they blind? Bats have wings and they can fly, but they are not flying mice. They are not blind, either. All bats have eyes, and all bats can see.

More than 2,500 years ago, the ancient Greeks knew that bats were not flying mice. In one of Aesop's fables, a bat falls and is caught by a weasel. The weasel says it will eat the bat because birds are its enemies, and the bat is the worst bird of all. The bat protests that it is not a bird, but a sort of flying mouse, and the weasel lets it go.

The bat falls again, and is caught by another weasel, who plans to eat it because he hates mice. The bat protests that it is not a mouse. It argues that it is not, in fact, a rodent at all, and again it escapes being eaten. The moral of Aesop's fable is to be flexible when faced by danger!

Not all bats are thought of as tricky or mysterious. Big bats called flying foxes live in Africa, Asia, and Australia. The face of a

GIGANTIC FLYING FOXES, ROOSTING HERE IN A TREE IN INDIA, SQUAWK NOISILY DURING THE DAY.

flying fox looks a lot like a dog's. They roost in trees, in the open where people can see them. No one is afraid of these big bats. Chinese fabrics and dishes are often decorated with bat-shaped designs for good luck. On some islands of the South Pacific, people eat these big bats at festivals, also for good luck.

IF A BAT FLIES INTO YOUR HOUSE

What should you do if there's a bat flying around in your house? Don't panic. Don't swat at it. It's probably young, and it's definitely lost. It wants to get out. Close the door of the room it's in, so you know where it is, and open a window. It will probably find its own way out.

If the bat settles down instead of flying out, you can probably catch it. First, put on gloves, just to be safe. A frightened bat may try to bite you, but with its tiny teeth and mouth, it can't bite through a leather glove. Then walk slowly up to the bat and cover it with a wastebasket or a big can. Slide a piece of cardboard between the container and the wall or floor. Keep the container covered and take it outside. Put the container on the ground and remove the cardboard. The bat will soon fly away.

If you have bat visitors more than once, inspect your house to see where they are getting in. Bats can squeeze through tiny openings. Look for tiny cracks and close them. Any hole bigger than a dime should be sealed. Tape works—unlike mice, bats won't chew through tape.

If a large colony is sharing your house and creating a real problem, don't let a pest-control company fill your house with poisons. You may damage your own health—and still have bats. Ultrasonic bat repellents don't work, either. The best solution is to wait for the bats to migrate and then inspect the house and seal up all their entrances. If you can wait until winter, when all the bats have gone, you will not risk trapping baby bats left in the roost while their mothers feed.

Bats as Neighbors

Whether we know it or not, many of us have bats living near us. Bats do not attack people, and they don't get tangled in our hair. If a bat swoops close to you outdoors, it is probably chasing an insect, and may even save you from a mosquito bite.

Towns and suburbs can be good habitats for bats. Many bats seem to think people build houses, barns, and churches to share with them. Big brown bats and little brown bats readily roost in attics and under porches. In the evening, you can often see them hunting in parks, around streetlights, or over ponds or swimming pools. Both species hibernate in the winter. And both are very adaptable.

Not everyone admires bats. Large groups of bats can be noisy and smelly. Bats get sick and carry diseases, too. But both of these things are true for any species of wildlife. The most serious disease a bat can get is rabies—a disease that can be fatal to humans. For years, people thought bats could carry rabies and spread it to other animals without being sick themselves, but this isn't true. A bat that has rabies dies within a short time. Since handling a dead bat could expose you to rabies, the rule is: Don't touch it. Don't let your dog or cat go near it. Let an animal control officer decide what to do.

A bat that you can catch is probably a sick bat. But most bats are healthy, and they can be good neighbors. They help control insects. In some places, they pollinate plants or help spread their seeds so new plants grow. People who study bats and work with them usually come to like them a lot.

2 Ancestors and Families

Dark, threatening clouds hid the moon. It was going to storm. But the bat was hungry and thirsty. It left the cave where it roosted and flew out in search of food and water. It drank from a nearby stream and then caught and ate a few moths.

Suddenly it started to rain. It poured! The bat was caught before it could reach the shelter of its cave. It got soaked and could not fly. It fell into a puddle and died. Rushing rainwater carried its body away. When it came to a stop, wedged against some rocks, sand and silt quickly covered it.

FIFTY MILLION YEARS LATER IN GERMANY, SCIENTISTS FOUND THE FOSSIL of this bat. Fossils are the remains of plants or animals that were alive millions of years ago. A fossil forms when minerals in sediment cover an organism, slowly seeping into it and turning it to stone. A fossil can be an entire plant or animal, or a small piece of it. A footprint or the pattern left by a leaf can be fossilized too.

THIS IS ONE OF THE OLDEST BAT FOSSILS EVER FOUND, AND ONE OF THE MOST COMPLETE. IT WAS FOUND IN THE WESTERN UNITED STATES, IN WYOMING.

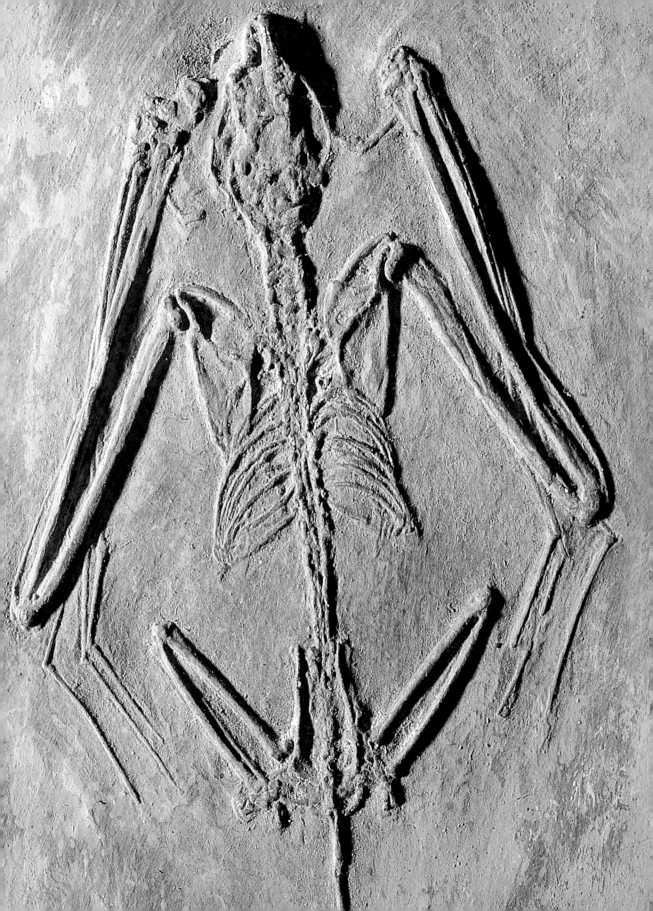

This bat fossil is one of the most complete ever found. Bats are tiny and their bones are delicate. Most bat fossils are just tiny fragments of bone or a few teeth. Complete or nearly complete bat fossils are rare. This one was so well preserved that scientists could see the bat had eaten moths shortly before it died. Did it really die in a rainstorm? We will never know.

What was the world like 50 million years ago? Scientists call that period in Earth's history the Eocene epoch. The climate was warm during the Eocene. Many of the plants growing then were similar to plants that grow now. Australia and Antarctica had become continents, separate from the giant supercontinent Pangaea.

The dinosaurs were gone. Large mammals, ancestors of whales and elephants, had appeared. They shared the planet with the early rodents and primates that had begun appearing about 10 or 15 million years before. Humans had not yet evolved as a species, and horses were tiny creatures with several toes. But bats were already bats.

Theories About Bat Evolution

The evolution of bats remains a puzzle. Fossils are the pieces, and we don't yet have enough of them to complete the picture. The first bat fossils ever found were unearthed less than one hundred years ago. Since then, fossils of bats have been discovered in Africa, Asia, Europe, and North and South America. We have the remains of about forty different species of bats. The oldest known bat fossils are about 60 million years old. We also have much more recent fossils from the Pleistocene—the last Ice Age. This was when our own species, *Homo sapiens*, evolved. These Ice Age fossils, which are about two million years old, include fossils of about one hundred species of bats that still exist today. Even the oldest known fossils are clearly recognizable as

The Evolution of Bats

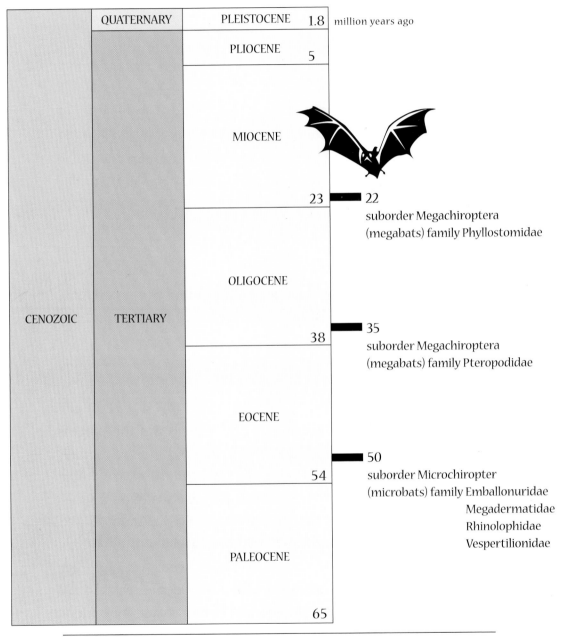

	QUATERNARY	PLEISTOCENE	1.8	million years ago
CENOZOIC		PLIOCENE	5	
		MIOCENE		
			23	■ 22
				suborder Megachiroptera (megabats) family Phyllostomidae
	TERTIARY	OLIGOCENE		
			38	■ 35
				suborder Megachiroptera (megabats) family Pteropodidae
		EOCENE		
			54	■ 50
				suborder Microchiropter (microbats) family Emballonuridae Megadermatidae Rhinolophidae Vespertilionidae
		PALEOCENE		
			65	

THE CENOZOIC ERA SPANS ABOUT 65 MILLION YEARS. MICROBATS EVOLVED EARLIER; MEGABATS MORE RECENTLY.

bats. These ancestors of today's bats had wings and could fly.

Scientists are sure that bats evolved from earlier mammals that did not fly. They are sure that their wings gradually evolved from more ordinary front legs and feet. Wings and flight must have begun evolving as early as 70 to 100 million years ago. But how did this happen?

The ancestors of bats were probably small tree-climbing mammals that jumped from branch to branch. Over millions of years, these animals may have developed membranes along the sides of their bodies that let them glide from tree to tree, as flying squirrels do now. Gradually, perhaps, the front toes of the animals that would become bats grew longer and membranes grew between their toes. While this was happening, their muscles adapted, or changed in a way that allowed their behavior to change. At this point—more than 60 million years ago—they had wings, could fly under their own power, and resembled the bats we know today.

There are two major groups of bats, megabats and microbats. One of the many unsolved scientific riddles is where megabats come from. The oldest megabat fossils are about 35 million years old. Did the megabats split off from existing bats and begin evolving separately sometime before that? Probably. Microbats and megabats are so much alike that it is reasonable to think they are very closely related. But scientists who have studied the structure of the brains of megabats suggest another possibility—that their closest relatives are not microbats at all, but primates.

Did megabats evolve from primitive primates? Did the ability to fly evolve twice, in two different mammals? It could have happened. Different animals sometimes develop similar characteristics. For example, some monkeys, some porcupines, and the Virginia opossum all have prehensile tails (tails that can grasp branches). Two groups of bats that are not closely related have developed long muzzles and tongues that enable them to feed on nectar.

Scientists are using a new tool—the ability to analyze the genetic structure of living things—to solve an old riddle. So far, DNA studies indicate that megabats and microbats shared an ancestor much more recently than either kind of bat shared an ancestor with a primate. But we don't yet have enough information to be certain.

We need much older fossils than any that have been discovered so far. Fossils of animals that were batlike, but not yet bats, would help solve the mystery. Fossils of mammals that were between megabats and microbats or between megabats and primates would confirm or contradict today's DNA evidence.

Will such fossils ever be found? Bat fossils tend to lie in cave deposits. Scientists first searched these deposits for big bones— the remains of dinosaurs and mammoths, for example. Now they are going back to these sites and screening for tiny fragments of bone and teeth. That is where most bat fossils are likely to turn up. Discoveries are made every year, on every continent. Perhaps you will make your own discovery someday.

Bats Are Classified

Humans like to name things. Maybe that's the way our brains have evolved. We like to figure things out. Naming things and figuring out how they are related to each other is what classification is all about. Scientists classify plants, animals, and even microbes. You can think about classification as putting together a giant puzzle. Each species is a piece of the puzzle. Where does it fit? Where do bats, as a group, fit?

Bats (and humans) are mammals. Like all mammals, they

BUILDING BLOCKS OF LIFE

All living things contain DNA—Deoxyribonucleic Acid. DNA forms the building blocks of genes, which are arranged in a specific sequence on the chromosomes of every species of plant and animal.

DNA forms the blueprint for most of the biochemical operations in our bodies. The complex structure of a living being is really the result of performing the operations that are encoded in DNA.

By examining the DNA of two different people, it is possible to determine if they are related. The same research can be done with animals or plants, making it possible to verify family trees and determine how closely one species is linked to another.

Scientists are comparing DNA sequences in different species of bats to help figure out evolutionary relationships. By determining differences and similarities in these sequences across many species of bats, it is possible to tell how long various species have been separated over the millions of years of geologic time.

DNA analysis often supports scientific conclusions based on older methods, such as examining the teeth and bone structure of fossil specimens and comparing those with living animals. Sometimes these new studies do not support earlier conclusions and force us to change our ideas about when different species evolved from a common ancestor, and therefore, how closely related they are.

are in the animal kingdom. They are in the phylum Chordata and the subphylum Vertebrata, meaning that they have spinal cords and skeletons inside their bodies. The Vertebrata, or vertebrates, are divided into classes: fish, amphibians, reptiles, birds, and mammals. Mammals can be very different from each other, but they have some important things in common. Mammals have hair, not feathers or scales. And female mammals produce milk to nourish their young.

There are more than 4,500 species of mammals in the world. Scientists divide them into orders. There are twenty-six orders, some with many species and others with only one or a few. Bats have an order all their own; they are the only mammals with wings, and the only mammals that can truly fly. Scientists classify them in the order Chiroptera. The name comes from two Greek words that together mean "hand-wing," because most of the bat's wing is supported by its extra-long hand and finger bones.

Bats are the second-largest order, after rodents. Scientists divide bats into two large groups called suborders. They divide these suborders into seventeen families. They divide the families into more than 175 genera and 900 species.

Bats and Microbats

Megabats—bats in the suborder Megachiroptera—all live in tropical climates and eat plant foods. The megabats that feed on fruit are commonly known as flying foxes, and the ones that eat nectar and pollen are often called blossom bats. They are also all known as Old World fruit bats.

As you might guess from the name, megabats tend to be bigger than microbats. The largest species of bat, the gigantic flying fox, is a megabat. This bat, from southeast Asia, can weigh

Buettikofor's epauletted bat, a megabat from West Africa, eats soft fruits such as bananas and figs. The large white patches on its shoulders, called epaulettes, show that this bat is a male.

than 3 pounds (about 1.5 kg). Its body is about the size of a football, only not quite as fat, and it can have a wingspan of more than 6 feet (about 2 m). Megabats have big eyes and faces like dogs (or foxes, which explains the name "flying fox"). There are 166 species of megabats, all in one family named Pteropodidae.

The other families of bats are in the suborder Microchiroptera. These are the microbats, the bats that we see in North and South America. Microbats live all over the world, but megabats are restricted to parts of Asia, Africa, and Australia.

The easiest way to recognize a megabat is to look closely at its wing. It has two claws, one on its thumb and one on its next finger. Microbats only have one claw, on the thumb. However, this difference is not enough to separate the megabats and assign them to their own suborder and family. Megabats also have much better-developed brains than microbats. They are probably better able to decide how to behave in different situations, instead of relying only on instinct. When hunting for food, they rely more on their senses, especially sight and smell, and less on sound waves, or echolocation. Another difference is that a roosting megabat bends its neck toward its chest and looks at the world upside down. A roosting microbat bends its neck toward its back and looks at the world right-side up.

Microchiropterans, or microbats, echolocate when they fly and hunt for food. Although they all can see, their eyes tend to be small and sometimes hidden in their fur. Most microbats eat insects, although some catch and eat larger prey such as lizards and even small mammals, and vampire bats live on blood. Microbats in one family, the Phyllostomidae, eat fruit, nectar, or pollen, as well as insects. This variety of food habits is accompanied by a variety of wing shapes and flight patterns. Because microbats are so varied, scientists divide them into sixteen families. Here are descriptions of ten of them, grouped according to where they are found in the world.

Microbats of Asia, the Middle East, Africa, and Australia

Hog-nosed bat (family Craseonycteridae). This family includes only one species, the hog-nosed bat. Among the lightest of the world's mammals, it has a 6-inch (15 cm) wingspan and weighs less than one-tenth of an ounce (0.07 oz, or about 2 grams). This bat was unknown to science until 1974, when it was discovered in Thailand. It eats insects.

Old World False Vampire bats and Yellow-winged bats (family Megadermatidae). These large bats are found in Africa, Asia, the East Indies, and Australia. Some of the five species eat vertebrates, but none live on blood, so "false vampire" is a misleading name. The Australian false vampire bat (also called the Australian ghost bat) is the largest microbat in the world.

Slit-faced bats (family Nycteridae). These bats have a dent in their skull, a sunken ridge that extends from their nostrils to a pit in the middle of their forehead. You can't see this in a living bat—the dent is hidden by fur. The function of this slit is unknown, but based on its location, scientists suspect that it is related to echolocation. The twelve species of slit-faced bats live in forest and savanna habitats in parts of Africa and Asia. They are relatively large and feed on big insects, snatching them from the ground or from leaves. Most roost in small groups in caves, hollow trees, rocks, or foliage.

Horseshoe bats and Roundleaf bats (family Rhinolophidae). Horseshoe bats have a complex, three-part nose. The bottom part is horseshoe-shaped, and the top part sticks up like a spear. When these bats echolocate, they send their ultrasonic signals through the nose instead of through the mouth like most bats. The sixty-four species are widespread in Europe, Asia, Africa, and Australia. When they roost—in caves, buildings, hollow trees, or sometimes in foliage—these bats often wrap their wings around their body and look like large cocoons.

Roundleaf bats, which have an elaborate flap of skin on the nose called a nose leaf, also echolocate by sending signals through the nose. Most are relatively small bats and all eat insects. They live in the tropics in Africa, Asia, and Australia.

Microbats Around the World

Sheath-tailed bats, Sac-winged bats, and Ghost bats (family Emballonuridae). Bats in this family have an unusual, short tail. Most of the tail is inside the tail membrane, like a sword in its sheath, but the tip of the tail pokes up through the top of the tail membrane. There are forty-eight species of sheath-tailed bats, some small and others quite large. They live in tropical and subtropical climates around the world. Four species, in Mexico, Central America, and South America, are white and are known as ghost bats. Other species have a little sac, a gland that secretes a liquid with a strong odor on the wings. We don't know why the bats have this gland. It is usually bigger in male bats, and may help them attract females.

Naked-backed bats and Mustached bats (family Mormoopidae). This family of insect-eating bats is found only in the Americas. They have wrinkled, funnel-shaped lips and small eyes. Two species are called naked-backed because their wing membranes, which are not fur-covered, meet in the middle of their back. Bats in this family usually roost in caves or tunnels, although some have been found in houses. They catch insects in the air rather than taking them from leaves or from the ground.

HERE ARE MICROBATS FROM FIVE DIFFERENT FAMILIES. THEIR FAMILY NAME, IN LATIN, IS FOLLOWED BY THEIR COMMON SPECIES NAME.

Megadermatidae: Australian ghost bat

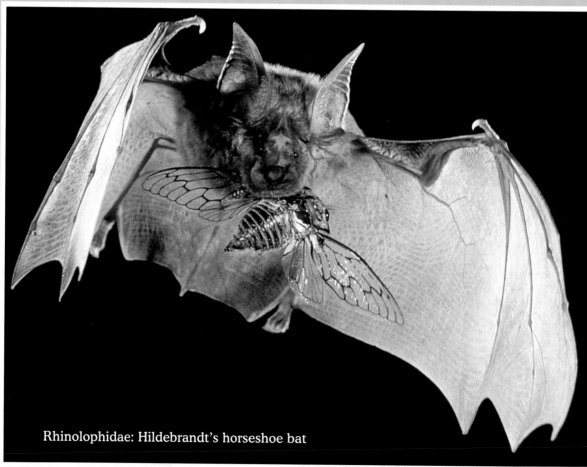

Rhinolophidae: Hildebrandt's horseshoe bat

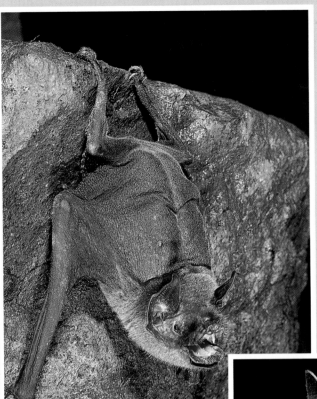

Phyllostomidae: tent-making bat

Mormoopidae:
naked-backed bat

Vespertilionidae:
red bat

New World leaf-nosed bats (family Phyllostomidae). This family includes the largest bats in the Western Hemisphere, spectral vampire bats. Their wingspan can reach about 3 feet (or nearly 1 meter). Contrary to what their name implies, they do not drink blood. They prey on birds, rodents, and other bats. They live in forests from Mexico to Brazil. They have large ears, large nose leaves, and broad wings. Vampire bats—the ones that really do live on blood—are in this family, as well.

Other bats in this huge family eat fruit or nectar. They include long-tongued and long-nosed bats, Caribbean flower bats, short-tailed fruit bats, epauletted bats, and tent-making bats. Epauletted bats are easily recognized because they have whitish spots on their shoulders. They live in forests, usually roost in hollow trees, and eat fruit. Tent-making bats make shelters by biting leaves so they form little tents.

Disk-winged bats (family Thyropteridae). A disk-winged bat can hang from a pane of glass with the suction-cuplike disks on its wrists or ankles. There are three species of these unusual bats, all in the tropics of Central and South America. Disk-winged bats roost in small groups in new, rolled-up leaves of banana and other tropical trees. The bats have to move frequently because the leaves unfurl in a day or two. These tiny bats are skilled at flying through the undergrowth of the rain forest when they hunt for insects, avoiding obstacles in their path.

Free-tailed bats (family Molossidae). Free-tailed bats sometimes live in huge colonies of up to 20 million individuals in one cave. When they all fly out at night to hunt for insects, they look like a huge black cloud rising into the sky. Exit flights of free-tailed bats are tourist attractions in some parts of the southwestern United States. Free-tailed bats are found worldwide in the tropics and subtropics. Their name comes from the fact that the tail is not enclosed in the tail membrane.

Vespertilionid bats (family Vespertilionidae). *Vesper* is the Latin word for evening, so you can think of this huge family of more than three hundred species as evening bats. Little brown bats, the bats most likely to roost in your attic, are vespertilionids. So are big brown bats and most other species common to North America

Bats in this family are found all over the world. They include brightly colored painted bats with long, curly fur, from African and Asian forests. Painted bats are quite variable, ranging from bold patterns of orange or scarlet mixed with black fur, through reddish and yellowish species to more dull-colored ones.

Long-fingered bats, which hunt for beetles and other flying insects in Africa, Asia, and islands in the Pacific Ocean, are also vespertilionidid bats. The name comes from elongated fingers that fold back upon themselves when the bats are at rest. They form huge nursery colonies in some areas and are known to be seasonally migratory as well.

Tube-nosed, insect-eating bats from Asia, which are also in the family Vespertilionidae, have striking tubelike extensions on their nostrils. They are good examples of how little we know about many species of bats. We don't know the reason for these curious nostrils. We know almost nothing about their evolutionary history. Even their everyday ecological requirements are almost entirely unknown. Species such as this live on every continent, leaving plenty of room for future bat biologists to learn more about them.

3

The Body of the Bat

The skeletons of bats and humans are remarkably similar. The most basic difference in body structure between you and a bat is that you are designed to walk, while bats are well-designed flying machines. To look closely at the similarities and differences, let's turn you into a bat. You will be a microbat, one that lives in the United States and Canada. Megabats, the big flying fox bats of Africa, Asia, and Australia, are very similar, so you'll be learning how their bodies work as well.

Your Arms and Hands

First, we'll make your arms much longer. Your shoulders and upper arms won't change a lot, but your forearms will grow quite long. Your human forearm is made of two almost equal bones. In your new bat forearm, one of the bones, the radius, will be much bigger and stronger than the other one. The second forearm

THE ARM, HAND, AND FINGER BONES OF THIS SHORT-TAILED FRUIT BAT ARE ETCHED AGAINST THE NIGHT SKY IN READINESS TO LAND ON A BUNCH OF RIPE BANANAS.

bone, the ulna, will be small. The ulnas will act as braces when you stiffen your elbows and spread your wings to fly. As a human, you can turn your arm so that the palm of your hand is up or down. As a bat, you will not be able to do this.

Your hand and finger bones will also get much longer because they will support your wings. Your little finger will become the longest of all. Except for your thumb, your hand and finger bones will be entirely inside your wings.

Your thumb will stick out, and it will have a claw. You will find it useful when you want to groom yourself. You can also hang by your thumbs. Since you won't want to defecate or urinate while you are hanging upside down, you'll spin around and hold on with your thumb claws.

Horseshoe Bat Skeleton

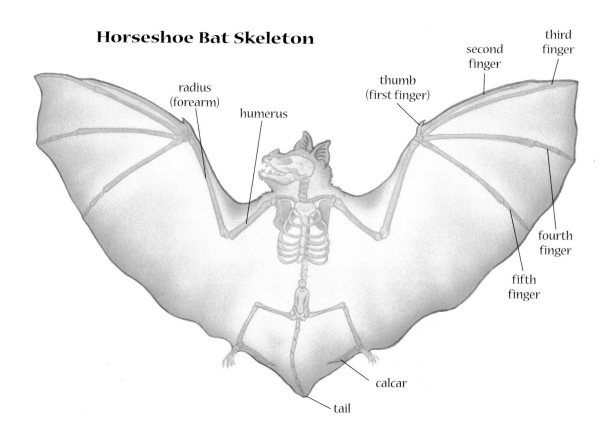

Your body will be widest and heaviest at your shoulders and much narrower at your hips than it is now. Your upper body has to support strong muscles on your chest and back that make it possible for you to flap your wings and fly.

Your Legs and Feet

As a bat, you won't really walk. Your legs can help you move a little on the ground, but that's not their main purpose. They will do two things for you: support your wings when you are flying and hold the weight of your body when you are hanging by your feet at your roost.

Your legs will be connected to your body differently. They will be turned far to the side, and your knees will bend toward your back. When you roost on a tree, your stomach will face the tree trunk and your knees will bend away from the tree. As a bat, you won't be able to bend your knees toward the front of your body. Sitting on a chair will no longer be possible.

Your feet will be small, with tiny, sharp claws on your toes. They are just what you need for roosting upside down, which is a great advantage. If you are in danger and have to fly away in a hurry, all you have to do is let go with your claws, drop, and start flapping your wings.

Your Wing and Tail Membranes

Your wings are two thin layers of skin. They are extensions of the skin that covers your body. These two layers will come all the way out to the end of your fingers. Your hand and arm bones will be inside these two layers of skin, which form your wing membrane. Only your thumb will stick out.

Your wings also have to be connected to your legs. Your

BATS' WINGS ARE MADE OF TWO THIN LAYERS OF SKIN STRETCHED OVER A
FRAMEWORK OF HAND AND FINGER BONES. THE BAT'S THUMB STICKS OUT FROM
THE WING MEMBRANE.

wing membrane starts at your shoulder and stretches out over
your hand and fingers all the way down to your ankle. Your
wings are only about as thick as a plastic sandwich bag—so thin
that light shines through them—and they feel somewhat rub-
bery. Even though they are thin, they are strong. Your wing
membrane won't tear easily if you snag it on a branch. You have
blood vessels in your wings, which can help you cool your body
when it is hot, but no flesh.

Another membrane stretches between your hind legs. A
spur of bone on each ankle, called a calcar, will help hold this
membrane in a good position for flying. Depending on what
kind of bat you are, your tail might be completely inside this
membrane, it might stick out, or you might not have a tail at all.

Your Neck and Head

Your neck will be short, but very flexible. When you are hanging upside down with your stomach against a tree, you can bend your neck back to see what's coming. Even though you are hanging upside down, you will be looking at the world right side up. You will have the same seven neck bones you had as a human, and as all other mammals have.

Now for your face. Bat faces range from sort of cute to really ugly. Some of the common names of bats will give you a hint about what they look like: There are hog-nosed bats, wrinkle-lipped bats and wrinkle-faced bats, tube-nosed bats, and dog-faced bats. There are leaf-nosed and sword-nosed and spear-nosed bats, among many others. What you eat and how you find your food will affect your appearance, the length of your jaw, and the number of teeth in your mouth. If you eat food you have to

Horseshoe Bat Body

dactylopatagium longus

dactylopatagium latus

uropatagium

plagiopatagium

chew, you will have more teeth than if you live on liquids such as nectar or blood. Your tongue might be long if you poke it into flowers to drink nectar, or short if you eat insects.

You'll have bright little eyes. Even though all bats can see, you do most of your flying at night. You will rely on a special navigation system, echolocation, to get around. You'll use your nose or mouth and your ears for that, so you don't need sharp eyesight. When you echolocate, you will make ultrasonic sounds with your larynx (your voice box) and listen for the echoes that bounce back to your ears.

Your ears might be relatively small, medium-sized, or huge. Many of the common names of bats tell you something about their ears: There are mouse-eared, small-eared, round-eared, big-eared, long-eared, funnel-eared, and trumpet-eared bats. Sometimes, you'll use your ears just as a human does; other times, you'll use them to receive your incoming echolocation signals.

The last thing to do is trade your clothing for a coat of fur. Your fur is one of the things that distinguishes you from all other classes of animals. All mammals have hair (fur is a kind of hair). Yours will be soft and silky. The pelage—a fancy name for fur—of most bats is black, brown, or gray, but there are red bats and yellow bats, spotted bats, striped bats, and even white bats.

How Will Your Body Work?

Bats are much like humans inside. Some organ systems work a little differently, though, since bats fly. Some help bats conserve energy when the weather is too hot or too cold. Others make it possible for them to echolocate.

Like all mammals, you'll have muscles. Some of yours will be special ones for moving your wings. Try flapping your arms. Did you move them up and down? If so, picture yourself flying

THE EARS OF TOWNSEND'S BIG-EARED BAT ARE NEARLY HALF AS LONG AS ITS BODY. THIS BAT, FROM SOUTHWESTERN CANADA, THE WESTERN UNITED STATES, AND MEXICO, EATS MOSTLY MOTHS. ITS HUGE EARS HELP IT DETECT AND CAPTURE ITS PREY.

and try again. When you fly, your body will be horizontal. Your wings will pull toward your chest as though you were clapping your hands. Can you feel your chest muscles pulling your hands toward your chest? Your bat muscles will give you a very big chest. They'll have a good blood supply to provide oxygen during the hard work of flight.

You'll have a nervous system: a brain, a spinal cord, and nerves. Your brain is relatively large for your small body size, and the part that processes sound, the auditory center, is especially well developed. You process echolocation signals here. Your cousins the megabats rely much more heavily on vision. Their brains have larger visual centers than yours and smaller auditory centers. Your spinal cord is larger in the upper part of your body and smaller in your lower body. It contains all of the nerves necessary to control your wings and chest muscles during flight.

Your heart will be big compared to the size of your body. It will beat much more rapidly than your human heart does when you are active and more slowly when you are resting. If you hibernate or go into a state of rest called torpor, it will slow

Horseshoe Bat Organs

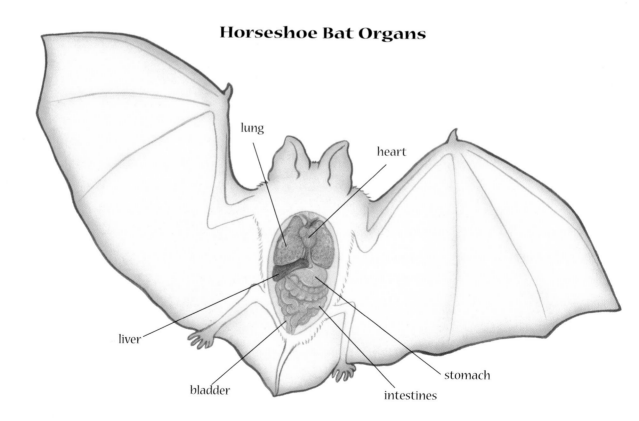

lung

heart

liver

bladder

intestines

stomach

down even more. Special valves let you regulate how much blood flows to the blood vessels in your wings. More blood will flow to the wings to cool you off when you are flying. The blood flow will slow down so you can stay warm when you are roosting. Other valves in your circulatory system make it possible for you to hang upside down. Did you—the human you—ever stand on your head or hang by your knees? If you did, blood rushed to your head and you may have felt dizzy. As a bat, you won't have that problem.

Your body will digest food very quickly. You will eat and then get rid of waste without delay. This helps you fly without carrying extra weight.

When you are an adult, you will mate and produce offspring. If you are a female, you will nurse your young. You will probably have just one baby each year, although some microbats have twins, and a few even have three or four pups at a time. You will probably have two nipples—most microbats do. You will have one nipple under each arm, near your armpit. When you are nursing your baby it will nestle safely under your wing.

4 Flight and Echolocation

A little brown bat flies to a stream in the woods to hunt. It woke up thirsty, so first it wants a drink. Without landing, it flies close to the surface of the water and dips its mouth for a drink. Then it starts its search for food. It darts back and forth among the leaves and branches that hang over the stream. It twists and turns in the air as it chases insects.

The bat flies with its mouth open, but not because it hopes a bug will fly in by accident. It is echolocating. It uses sound the way you use sight: to find out what is around it and decide what direction to go next. It catches its prey in the air without ever bumping into a branch or another bat.

BATS, SUCH AS THIS LITTLE BROWN BAT, HUNT AT NIGHT, USING ECHOLOCATION TO HELP THEM FIND THEIR PREY.

Flight and echolocation make bats special. All bats can fly. No other mammals have wings, and no other mammals can fly. Echolocation is a superb navigation system that makes it possible for bats to fly and hunt in the dark.

Flight

Bats fly under their own power. Flying squirrels, flying lemurs, and Australian gliders can climb up high, launch themselves into the air, and sail down to a lower place, but they aren't really flying. They are gliding. Birds are the only other vertebrates that can fly. It's much easier to see birds flying than bats because most birds are diurnal (active during the day). When stop-action photography was invented, scientists were able for the first time to see how bats move their wings when they swerve and turn.

Watch birds fly. How many different styles of flight can you identify? If you are lucky enough to see a flock of Canada geese migrating, notice how these big, heavy birds never stop beating their wings. Brown pelicans look big and heavy, too, but they can sail along just above the surface of the water for quite a distance without moving their wings. Watch a crow take off from the roof of a house. It jumps forward into the air, and as it starts to fall, it flaps its wings. It uses both gravity and the power of its strong wings to take flight. Some birds use their wings to gain airspeed, and then coast for a short (or long) distance. Others flutter their wings the whole time they are airborne. Hummingbirds' wings move so rapidly when they are hovering in front of a flower that you can't see them.

Bats have different styles of flight, too. Some nectar-eating bats are almost as good as hummingbirds at hovering to feed from plants. Bats that feed on insects high in the air are often

BATS AND BIRDS

Bats and birds are not closely related, and they developed flight independently. While some differences are easy to see, others are not. Here are ways in which they differ:

Bats	Birds
All can fly	Not all birds can fly (emus, ostriches, penguins)
Give birth to live young	Lay eggs; young hatch from eggs
Nurse their young with milk from the mother's body	Bring food to their young
Do not build nests	Many build nests
Have fur	Have feathers
Have teeth	Have beaks; do not have teeth
Have marrow-filled bones	Have hollow bones
Hand and finger bones support the wings	Arm bones support the wings
Leg bones help support the wings	Leg bones do not support the wings
None live in (or on) water	Some live in (or on) water
Some hibernate	None hibernate
Most are nocturnal	Most are diurnal
Most are quiet	Many are noisy
Most are not brightly colored	Many are brightly colored

A SOUTHERN
LONG-NOSED BAT
HOVERS TO LICK
THE FRUIT OF AN
ORGAN-PIPE CACTUS.

fast, direct flyers. Other insectivorous (insect-eating) bats hunt in dense foliage and have perfected the art of slow, maneuverable flight. No bird can twist and turn in the air the way these bats do when they are chasing flying insects. One of the big megabats, the Samoan flying fox, can soar like a bird, riding on currents of air. But more typically, bats beat their wings the entire time they are flying.

Taking Off and Staying Up

Birds, bats—and airplanes—all need air flowing past their wings to take off and stay airborne. Airplanes gain airspeed by taxiing down a runway. Birds create a flow of air that lets them take off by flapping their wings. A few species of bats—for instance, vampire bats, which are able to take off from the ground—can gain enough speed to fly by leaping upward and flapping their wings. However, most bats start flying by dropping into the air from a roosting place. As they drop into flight, they flap their wings to level off and move forward.

Things that fly—living things as well as airplanes—stay airborne because air is flowing faster over the wings than it is flowing under the wings. This differential in airspeed above and below the wing creates a pressure difference that results in lift. Lift is what overcomes the pull of gravity and allows the bat to remain airborne.

The length and shape of the wing, the weight of the body, and where the weight is in relation to the wings all determine the amount of energy needed to stay in the air. Lift is also affected by the pattern of airflow over the wing. Wings that minimize friction generate faster airflow above, greater pressure differential, and more lift. So most bat wings are very smooth on top.

In addition to lift, some form of thrust is necessary for true powered flight. Bats generate thrust by flapping their wings in both an up-and-down and a front-to-back motion, somewhat as humans swim the butterfly stroke. The combination of lift and thrust allows a bat to remain aloft. Without enough airspeed, the bat, bird, or airplane stalls.

Big brown bats have been made to fly in a wind tunnel of a laboratory, where their speed can be measured. They were clocked at 15 miles (24 km) per hour in this kind of test. Chances are the bats can fly faster in their natural environment than they did in the laboratory.

Wing Shape and Lifestyle

Wing shape and lifestyle go together. Bats that forage high in the air and fly long distances have long, narrow wings. The western mastiff bat flies high—it forages for insects as much as 2,000 feet (610 m) above the ground. It easily covers long distances, flying as far as 15 miles (24 km) from the nearest roost, a 30-mile (48 km) nonstop round-trip, in addition to the miles it flies while it is hunting. Western mastiffs hunt high over the treetops or in open country. They make spectacular dives, partly folding their wings and plummeting downward. Then they spread their wings and level out to continue their journey or to swoop up to a roosting place.

Bats with shorter, broader wings, such as the little brown bat, don't fly as fast. They specialize in maneuverable flight. They can hunt in dense woods or close to the ground, in and around shrubs. Little brown bats catch all their food in the air. Other species of bats with short, broad wings hover over a tasty morsel and then snatch it from a leaf or from the ground. The high-flying western mastiff bat can't take off from a flat surface, but these bats can.

BATS' WINGS COME IN MANY SHAPES AND SIZES. LONG, NARROW WINGS ARE BEST FOR SWIFT, DIRECT FLIGHT, AND SHORTER, BROADER WINGS MAKE SLOW, HOVERING FLIGHT POSSIBLE.

A fruit bat in flight

A greater horseshoe bat chasing a moth

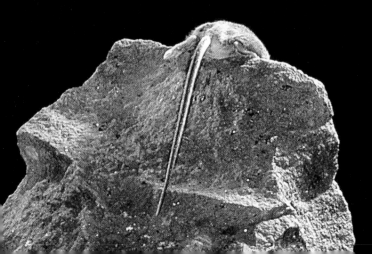

A false vampire bat
descending on its prey

Echolocation

All insect-eating bats echolocate when they are hunting, and all microbats use echolocation to navigate. When a bat echolocates, it makes sounds with its larynx (voice box). Usually the sounds are ultrasonic, meaning that they are above the range of human hearing.

The sounds come out of the bat's mouth or nose. Different species of bats have different ways of emitting the sound. When the sound waves hit objects in the bat's environment, they bounce back. From the echoes that bounce back to its ears, the bat gets a good enough picture in its brain to hunt successfully or find its way safely to a roost deep inside a dark cave. In total darkness, owls crash into walls. Bats don't. Even in daylight, birds sometimes crash into glass windows, but bats can detect glass and avoid it.

Bats broadcast sound in short pulses, not in one long, continuous hum. A little brown bat searching for prey may make about twenty calls per second. When it has found an insect and is chasing it, the bat calls as often as two hundred times per second. This is called a "feeding buzz."

If the sound is ultrasonic, how do we know the bat is making a sound? An early high-tech invention—a microphone that could pick up sounds the human ear cannot hear and translate them into signals within the range of human hearing—first let humans hear bats echolocate about sixty years ago. Before that, some scientists suspected bats were using sound to navigate, but they couldn't prove it. Today, researchers use much more sensitive microphones, sometimes attached to computers, to study the high-tech navigation system of bats. These devices are called bat detectors.

Anyone who looks at the face of a leaf-nosed bat might ask, "What are these lumps and bumps supposed to do?" Scientists

ULTRASOUND: A KIND OF ECHOLOCATION

What does a bat "see" when it echolocates? Does it have an actual picture of its surroundings in its brain? We know that an echolocating bat can chase and catch a tiny insect. While it is flying at top speed, it also avoids branches, other flying bats, and you, if you are walking where it is hunting.

A medical sonogram, or ultrasound, produces a picture using a kind of machine-made echolocation. Ultrasonic sound waves are directed into—and through—the body of the patient. The sound waves travel through fluid and through the soft tissue of the body, but not through air or bone. Echoes bounce back from inside the body, producing a computer picture.

A sonogram is not a still picture, like an X ray. It shows the internal organs at work. It can show a heart beating or kidneys filling and emptying. An echolocating bat knows what is moving around it while it, too, is moving. But we don't yet know whether the bat receives an image in its brain in the same way the computer creates an image on a screen. Perhaps you will be the one to make this connection.

This round-eared bat sends its echolocation signals through its nose. Its nose leaf helps direct the outgoing signal. The ultrasonic signal hits an insect and bounces back to the bat's huge ears, enabling the bat to identify and catch its prey.

are still working on the answer. Strong evidence suggests that the decorations on some bats' noses (nose leafs) are linked to echolocation. Bats that emit their echolocation calls through their nostrils have nose leaves. They probably help send signals in the right direction.

Many species of bats also have one or two flaps of skin where their ears open. These are called a tragus and antitragus. They probably affect the way the returning echoes come into the ears, helping the bats get accurate information as they fly and echolocate.

Old World fruit bats, the megabats also known as flying foxes, don't echolocate the way microbats do. Some of them echolocate by making clicking sounds with their tongues, but they do not rely on echolocation to navigate or find food. Flying foxes leave their roosts before dark, flapping their big wings slowly and sometimes soaring. They rely on vision and smell to find trees full of ripe fruit.

5 Roosting and Finding Food

If you are walking in the woods on a nice summer day and look up and think you see a dead leaf, you might be right. But you might be wrong. You may have spotted a red bat. Red bats summer in southern Canada and the United States. They roost alone in the foliage.

At the other extreme, Brazilian free-tailed bats are never alone. An estimated 20 million of them roost together in one cave in Texas. When they all leave the cave in the evening to forage for insects, they look like a great dark cloud rising into the sky. Another large colony lives in summer under a bridge in Austin, Texas.

Western mastiff bats have to find roosts that are open at the bottom. They are big bats, with long, narrow wings, and cannot take off from a flat surface. The western mastiff bat has to free-fall to get up enough speed to fly. If it is on the ground it will scramble up a tree to get the height it needs for a successful launch. Its usual roost is a deep crack in the rocks in a rugged

MOST BATS ROOST IN GROUPS EITHER WITH ONLY A FEW OTHER BATS OR IN COLONIES OF THOUSANDS OR EVEN MILLIONS. HOARY BATS (INSET) AND RED BATS ARE UNUSUAL: THEY ROOST ALONE.

canyon. Sometimes a small group of western mastiff bats shares the same crevice.

Flying foxes roost in trees out in the open. In Australia, a tree full of hundreds of flying foxes—or many trees full of thousands of them—is called a camp. You might live near bats all your life and never know it, but if you live near a camp of flying foxes, you know the bats are there. They squawk noisily during the day, and the area around a large camp has a strong odor.

Why Do Bats Roost?

Bats use roosts for different reasons. Day roosts are places to sleep. Caves are the most widely used day-roosting sites. Other choices can be crevices in rocks, hollow trees, the space under the bark of a tree, or a quiet, dark place in a building. It depends on what kind of bat is seeking shelter, and what kind of shelter it can find.

Unless they roost in large numbers near people, people often don't know that bats are living nearby. A few bats living behind the shutters of a house or in an attic often don't attract attention. Large colonies make things more complicated. Bats may help control insects, but guano (bat droppings) piling up in an attic can make even a bat-loving homeowner unhappy.

Night roosts offer a place to rest between foraging flights. Some bats, such as fruit-eating bats, may use night roosts as a place to feed. So do bats that eat large prey. They prefer flying to a roost where they can swallow their food in private. If they eat in the open they are in danger of becoming food themselves—for an owl, for instance.

Many species of female bats use nursery roosts to give birth and raise their young until they are old enough to fly. Nursery roosts can contain just a few mothers or thousands of them. The

Brazilian free-tailed bat may be the record holder: As many as three thousand baby bats may cling to 3 square feet (1 sq m) of a cave's ceiling. Hundreds of thousands of baby bats hang together in some large colonies, keeping each other warm. Not all bats use nursery roosts, though. Red bats, which live alone, raise their offspring alone, too.

Bats that hibernate through cold winters need a special kind of roost. They have to find a hibernaculum (a place to hibernate) where they will not be disturbed. It has to be cold, but above freezing. Caves, mine shafts, or unheated attics can all be good places to hibernate. Species that hibernate often use the same cave every winter and return to the same summer roost year after year.

DROPS OF MOISTURE CONDENSE ON THE FUR OF THESE LITTLE BROWN BATS HIBERNATING IN A CAVE IN PENNSYLVANIA. THEY WILL BE FINE UNTIL SPRING IF THEY ARE NOT DISTURBED.

Fish-Eating Bats

If you have an aquarium, try this experiment: Close your eyes and see if you can hear the ripples a fish makes when it swims near the surface. The greater bulldog bat can do that. The bat flies low over a pond or stream and uses echolocation to detect ripples in the water. Experiments have shown that the bat can tell which way a fish is moving and how fast it is going. The bat

THE FISHING BAT'S LEGS REFLECT IN THE WATER AS IT TRIES TO HOOK A FISH. WHEN IT DOES, IT WILL SWOOP THE FISH INTO ITS MOUTH AND EITHER EAT IT IN FLIGHT OR CARRY IT TO A ROOST TO EAT.

detects the fish, swoops down and snags it with its claws, and uses its tail membrane to whip the fish up into its mouth.

The greater bulldog uses its tail membrane to swoop the fish forward and up into its mouth. It might eat the fish in flight or carry it back to a perch to feed itself or its offspring. Its cheek pouches make good shopping bags for bringing food home for dinner. Greater bulldog bats, which live in Central and South America, can catch fish as large as 3 inches (8 cm) long.

Fishing bats hunt over rivers, lakes, and saltwater lagoons as well as ponds and streams. The greater bulldog bat's huge feet and claws dramatically reflect its lifestyle. Most adaptations are not as obvious, but you can often learn something about a bat's behavior just by looking at it. Its wings, face, and teeth usually tell you something about what it eats and how it hunts.

Insect-Eaters

Many bats—in fact, most bats—eat insects. Bats in thirteen families around the world catch them in midair. These bats are called aerial insectivores—aerial refers to the air, and insectivores refers to what they eat. Some aerial insectivores fly for hours at a time, using echolocation to chase and catch prey high above the treetops or over fields. Others hunt in and among the tree branches, darting and weaving as they fly. Typically, bats that hunt high in the air have long, narrow wings and bats that forage in the leaves, where they have to steer around things in their path, have short, broad wings.

Foliage-gleaning bats eat insects, too, but they don't catch them in the air. They pick them off leaves or from the ground. They prey on flying insects that have landed or insects that don't fly. Some species prey on large arthropods such as centipedes or scorpions. Some foliage gleaners have big ears and can hear sounds made by their prey, such as the fluttering wings of a moth or the scratching sounds made by a crawling scorpion.

Some of these bats keep flying while they are hunting. Others roost and wait for an insect to come their way. When they have captured an insect, they often fly to a feeding perch to eat it. They eat the body and let the wings drop to the ground. If you see a little pile of insect wings on the ground under a tree, you may be under last night's feeding perch.

Bats eat enormous quantities of food. The 20 million bats that summer in Bracken Cave, Texas, may eat about 495,000 pounds (225 metric tons) of insects in one night. Nursing mother bats use a tremendous amount of energy producing milk for their young. Each nursing Brazilian free-tailed bat eats more than its own weight in insects every night.

Other Prey for Bats

Many insect-eating bats are tiny. Fishing bats and other bats that catch and eat vertebrates (animals with backbones, including fish) are much larger. The Australian ghost bat is big enough to prey on mice. These bats use echolocation when they hunt, but they also use their eyes. When the bat sees a mouse or other small mammal, it swoops down and wraps the victim in its wings. It kills its prey by biting it, and then flies with it to a feeding roost. Australian ghost bats eat anything they can catch: large insects, frogs, lizards, and birds. They even prey on smaller bats. Vampire bats also use vertebrates, mostly cattle and birds, as a source of food; they live on their blood.

THE AUSTRALIAN GHOST BAT QUICKLY KILLS ITS PREY, THEN FLIES TO A SAFE ROOSTING PLACE. FEW BATS ARE BIG ENOUGH TO PREY ON MICE; MOST EAT INSECTS.

Two families of bats include species that eat fruit. Old World fruit bats are megabats in the family Pteropodidae. The fruit-eating bats that live in North and South America are microbats in the family Phyllostomidae.

Try eating a piece of fruit like a fruit bat. Take a bite of the fruit. Chew it and chew it, then use your tongue to press it against the roof of your mouth. Swallow the juice and—politely, of course—spit out the pulp that remains. If you were a fruit bat, you would have gotten all the nourishment out of the fruit, but you wouldn't have to fly with the extra weight of the pulp in your stomach.

If the fruit has one big seed, gnaw around it and drop the seed to the ground under your roost. If you have swallowed tiny seeds, chances are they will pass through your system as you fly. Either

An epauletted bat feasts on a mango. Like other African fruit bats, it often migrates short distances to find ripe fruit.

THE GREATER SHORT-NOSED FRUIT BAT, HERE ON A BANANA FLOWER, SPREADS
POLLEN AS IT MOVES FROM PLANT TO PLANT IN SEARCH OF RIPE FRUIT.

way, you are helping spread the seeds so that new plants grow.

Jamaican fruit bats eat fruit and also drink nectar. They visit
balsa trees, drink the nectar from the blossoms, and while they
are doing so, pollinate the plants. If you have ever built a balsa-
wood model, you can probably thank a bat: Balsa trees in Central
and South America depend on bats for pollination. Without the
bats, there would be no balsa tree harvest.

Bats don't change their environment the way humans and
beavers do. They don't build nests, as tree squirrels or birds do,
although in tropical Central and South America, some tiny bats
bite leaves to make them fold over into little tents they use for
shelter. Bats pretty much take the world as they find it. If the
resources they need are there, if they can find food and shelter,
they quietly go about the business of living.

6　Life Cycles

Thousands of baby bats hang from the ceiling of a cave. They don't know it, but to fall would mean death. Their mothers hung them there by the tiny, sharp claws on their feet almost as soon as they were born. The babies are pink: They have no fur yet to cover their skin. Their eyes are tightly closed.

These are gray bats. The babies are packed together in a limestone cave in the southeastern United States. The female bats give birth in the same caves year after year. The cave is warm (55–79° F, or 13–26° C) and moist. There is a river nearby.

It's spring. The adult bats mated last fall. Sperm stayed in the uterus of the female during the winter, while she hibernated. Early in the spring, an egg was fertilized, and a baby bat started to develop. When the pregnant female bats emerged from hibernation, they migrated back to the caves they had used the summer before. Places where groups of female bats give birth and raise their young are called nursery colonies or maternity colonies.

WARM AND SAFE IN ITS MOTHER'S WINGS, A GAMBIAN EPAULETTED FRUIT BAT PUP LICKS ITS LIPS—PERHAPS AFTER NURSING. MALE EPAULETTED BATS SEEM TO PLAY NO ROLE IN RAISING THEIR OFFSPRING.

As with most bat species, each mother gray bat has just one baby each year. When the mother bats fly out to forage for insects, they leave the babies hanging together in the cave. The babies will nurse for about a month. By July, when they are ready to fly and find food for themselves, insects will be plentiful. Then the colony will break up. All the bats, adult and young, will concentrate on getting fat. They have to store enough fat in their bodies to survive the winter, when they will hibernate.

Many temperate-climate, insect-eating bats give birth in nursery colonies. Nursery colonies can be huge or small. No one knew where Indiana bats raised their offspring until 1974, when a nursery colony of thirty bats was found under the loose bark of a dead tree.

Male gray bats and females without offspring also roost in colonies in the summer. They usually choose different caves from the ones where nursery colonies are located. Their summer caves are usually near a river, too, where the bats can forage for insects over water. Most caves used by gray bats in the summer are in Alabama, Tennessee, Kentucky, and Missouri.

When Autumn Comes

In September, about 1.6 million gray bats—thought to be the total population of this species—will migrate. They will fly hundreds of miles to the caves where they hibernate. If they survive the trip, they will spend the winter in one of nine caves.

They will stay in these cold caves (42–52° F, or 6–11° C) until late March or early April before starting the trip back to their summer roosts. In their second summer, young male and female bats will be old enough to mate and produce offspring.

When they are hibernating, their bodies almost shut down. Their breathing and heartbeats slow. Their temperature drops to

As few as fifteen or as many as several thousand Eastern horseshoe bats may use the same nursery cave. The pups will continue to nurse for another two to three weeks before they are weaned and begin to hunt for insects on their own. They will reach adult size in five to six weeks.

BATS

A bat is born
Naked and blind and pale.
His mother makes a pocket of her tail
And catches him. He clings to her long fur
By his thumbs and toes and teeth.
And then the mother dances through the night
Doubling and looping, soaring, somersaulting—
Her baby hangs on underneath.
All night, in happiness, she hunts and flies.
Her high sharp cries
Like shining needlepoints of sound
Go out into the night and, echoing back,
Tell her what they have touched.
She hears how far it is, how big it is,
Which way it's going:
She lives by hearing.
The mother eats the moths and gnats she catches
In full flight; in full flight
The mother drinks the water of the pond
She skims across. Her baby hangs on tight.
Her baby drinks the milk she makes him
In moonlight or starlight, in mid-air.
Their single shadow, printed on the moon
Or fluttering across the stars,
Whirls on all night; at daybreak
The tired mother flaps home to her rafter.
The others all are there.
They hang themselves up by their toes.
They wrap themselves in their brown wings.
Bunched upside-down, they sleep in air.
Their sharp ears, their sharp teeth, their quick sharp faces
Are dull and slow and mild.
All the bright day, as the mother sleeps,
She folds her wings about her sleeping child.

from *The Bat-Poet*, Randall Jarrell

about the temperature of the air around them. In this way, they save energy and can usually survive the winter on the fat stored in their bodies. If something disturbs them, they have to use a lot of energy to wake up, warm up, and fly to safety. Depending on how much fat they were able to store before hibernation, they may or may not survive. Because almost all the gray bats in North America are thought to hibernate in just nine caves, they need protection to survive as a species.

Other Bats and Their Life Stories

We know more about the lives of gray bats than we do about most species. There are more than nine hundred species of bats. And each has its own life story.

Like gray bats, hoary bats mate in the fall, and the pups are born in spring or early summer. Hoary bats live alone and raise their offspring alone. Unlike most bats, they usually have twins and may have a litter of three or four.

Most microbats are born without any fur, but newborn hoary bats have a coat of fine, silvery-gray hair, except on their bellies. The fur helps protect them from cold or wet weather since they are not being raised in a warm cave surrounded by other warm little bodies.

Red bats also have four nipples and often have twins. During the day, when the mother roosts with her babies, they snuggle next to her. They hold onto the roost she is using with one foot and onto their mother with the other foot. When the mother bat goes out to forage at night, she leaves them hanging from a twig or leaf. Curiously, although they are like hoary bats in many ways, their babies are born without any fur.

Bats grow up quickly. Little brown bats can fly before they are three weeks old. They begin to eat insects at about the same

RED BATS ROOST ALONE IN FOLIAGE. WHEN THE MOTHER BATS FLIES OFF TO
HUNT FOR INSECTS, SHE LEAVES HER OFFSPRING HANGING FROM A BRANCH LIKE A
DEAD LEAF.

time. They eat their first insects while they are still nursing. It may be that the mother bat brings them to the baby, but they are soon hunting for their own food. Red bats can fly when they are just over a month old.

Often, male and female bats lead largely separate lives, except when they come together to mate. Some, though, such as the yellow-winged bats of the African savanna, live in male-female pairs. They have their babies at the end of the dry season or the beginning of the wet season. During the wet season, there are huge numbers of insects. Mother bats who are nursing their young and need extra food, and young bats who are just beginning to hunt for themselves, have an abundant supply.

Adult yellow-winged bats often hunt by hanging from a branch and waiting for a likely insect to fly past, and then swooping down to catch it. For the first few weeks after it is born, the baby bat clings to its mother even when she is foraging. When it is just beginning to fly, it practices by holding onto its mother's neck with its feet and flapping its wings. The young bat stays with its parents for about a month after it has stopped nursing and can hunt by itself.

Mother bats seem to respond to distress cries of their young. A scientist studying frogs in Ecuador discovered a small bat clinging to a twig and put it in a cloth bag he was carrying. Soon another bat was clinging to the outside of the bag. He put it in the bag, too. When the bag was opened, the smaller bat was nursing. Probably the mother had left it while she hunted for food and heard its ultrasonic cries, which the scientist couldn't hear, when it was caught.

Solving the Problem of Winter

Gray bats live in a temperate climate, so they have to solve the problem of what to do in the winter. First they migrate, then they hibernate.

We don't always know what bats do in the winter. Silver-haired bats probably migrate. They are seen in forests and grasslands throughout much of the United States and southern Canada in the summer. In the spring and fall, when bats migrate, they have been found roosting on the sides of buildings, beneath the bark of trees or in tree cavities, and sometimes in caves. But few have ever been seen in the winter. If they migrate, where do they go? Do they hibernate? And if so, where?

The Brazilian free-tailed bats that summer in huge colonies in Texas and New Mexico do not hibernate. When fall comes, they migrate to a warmer climate where insects are still plentiful. They travel as far as 800 miles (1,287 km) to central and southern Mexico. Between February and April, they begin the long trip north again.

Much smaller colonies of Brazilian free-tailed bats also live in California, southern Oregon, and the southeastern United States. Instead of migrating, they stay there year-round and hibernate during cold weather.

Indiana bats hibernate. Between November and the middle of March, thousands of them hang together in cool, humid caves and abandoned mines. They are so close to each other that from below, you can only see their ears, noses, mouths, and wrists.

The bats leave their summer roosts and start migrating to the caves where they hibernate as early as the end of August. For a few weeks after they arrive, large numbers of bats fly in and out of the caves all night long.

The bats seem to spend the summer in widely scattered small groups, and then come together in large groups to hibernate. When they are swarming around the cave entrances in the fall, they may be choosing mates and mating. They are also busy

FREE-TAILED BATS ARRIVE IN TEXAS IN MARCH AND DEPART FOR MEXICO IN OCTOBER.

eating, putting on an extra bit of fat, enough to last them through the winter.

Life Span

Bats live much longer than other, equally small mammals. Mice and shrews often live less than two years, whereas microbats have been known to live as long as thirty years. Gray bats have been known to live as long as eighteen years, but their average lifespan is far shorter. Information about life span comes from bats that were banded as babies and recaptured many years later and from bats living in captivity.

7 Looking to the Future

Woolly bats are so small and delicate that some African woolly bats roost in empty nests made by weaver birds. They are called woolly bats because their fur is long and curly. They are also called painted bats because some of them are brightly colored. One Asian species has bright red or orange fur on its body and beautiful black and orange wings. Woolly bats have long, pointed, funnel-shaped ears.

There are twenty-two species of woolly bats. They live in tropical forests in Africa and southeast Asia. One species lives in Australia. Of the twenty-two, one African species is probably extinct. Five others, including the bright bat with orange and black wings, might soon be facing extinction. As for the remaining sixteen species, no one knows.

What do we know about woolly bats? We know what they

LITTLE IS KNOWN ABOUT MANY SPECIES OF BATS, INCLUDING THIS WESTERN MASTIFF. WE NEED TO LEARN MORE ABOUT BATS IN ORDER TO SAVE THEM FROM EXTINCTION.

look like and where they have been seen. What don't we know? Almost everything else.

Woolly bats have been seen flying close to the ground, late in the evening. They are probably all insect-eaters. The woolly bats caught in Australia were in dense vegetation, so scientists suspect they feed by gleaning, flying slowly among the leaves and plucking their food from surfaces rather than catching it in the air. Their short, broad wings support this hypothesis. Scientists examined their droppings and the contents of their stomachs and found evidence that the bats eat a lot of spiders. They may pluck the spiders from their webs.

Female bats captured in spring and early summer had finished nursing. When did they breed? When did they have their babies? Do they have just one baby, or twins? Do they use nursery colonies? All these questions and others remain unanswered.

Scientists think Australian woolly bats—called golden-tipped bats because their long brown fur has orange-gold tips, and they have golden fur on their forearms and thumbs—live only in forests along the east coast of Australia. These are moist, thick forests where there is heavy rainfall in the summer.

The first golden-tipped bat known to science was caught in 1878 in New Guinea, an island north of Australia. A few more were caught in Australia in 1884 and 1897. Eighty-four years passed. Finally, in 1981, scientists began using new kinds of bat traps. Since then about fifty of these rare bats have been captured. Gradually, we will learn their secrets. The trick is to learn enough about them to save them if they are in danger of extinction. A North American bat, Underwood's mastiff bat, is found in southern Arizona in the summer. Male and female bats have been captured in mist nets stretched over pools of water in the desert. Nothing is known about where the bats roost in the daytime or where they are when the weather is cold.

THIS HARP TRAP IS A RECENT INVENTION. HARPLIKE STRINGS STRETCHED OVER A
FRAME SNAG BATS WITHOUT HARMING THEM.

Studying Bats

Studying bats is much easier than it used to be. Mist nets were
developed about fifty years ago. They made it possible to catch
bats without hurting them. New kinds of traps have been invented, too. One kind is called a harp trap. It has strings, like a harp,

above a bag. Harp traps are placed where bats have to fly through a small opening, such as the entrance to a cave. A bat flying in or out of its roost can get tangled in the strings and drop down into the bag. It is very annoyed, but not hurt.

Bats captured this way can be examined in the laboratory. A scientist studying how bats hibernate can fit a bat with a tiny instrument that measures its heartbeat, body temperature, and other bodily functions. Then the temperature of its cage is gradually lowered until the bat enters into hibernation. Scientists can measure how much energy bats use while they are hibernating and how much it takes for them to wake up if they are disturbed. Knowing what bats need is a crucial step toward saving whole species from extinction.

Studying bats in the wild is easier now, too. Captured bats can be fitted with tiny radio tags and then released. Bat detectors let scientists listen to echolocation calls.

What Does the Future Hold?

Many people are afraid of bats. Yet, in truth, bats are the ones who should be afraid of people. People hurt or kill bats on purpose and sometimes by accident. Bats have been killed by people who are afraid of them or fear the diseases they carry. In Australia, people built a school right next to trees where fruit bats had roosted for more than one hundred years. Then the people started complaining about how noisy and smelly the bats were.

The good news is that more and more people care about bats and want to save them.

Bats have always roosted in caves. They find mines almost as good for roosting. Old mines used to be sealed up or blasted away to protect people from falling into mine shafts. Now they

GATES PLACED OVER THE MOUTH OF CAVES PROTECT HIBERNATION SITES FOR BATS.

are often fitted with big metal gates that keep people out but let bats come and go. Scientists are studying how individual species of bats respond to different kinds of gates so they will be bat-friendly. Caves, too, can be protected by gates. Bats can hibernate without being disturbed and raise their young safely in gated caves and mines. Some caves where large colonies of gray bats hibernate are now protected by gates.

Loss of habitat is a serious threat. Natural disasters such as wildfires and floods can destroy bat habitats. So can elephants that tear down trees. But the most serious threat comes from humans. When a forest is cut down, habitat disappears. When a new housing development is built, habitat disappears. When a cave becomes a tourist attraction, habitat disappears.

Are some species of bats in danger of extinction? A recent list of nine hundred species of bats lists three hundred of these as stable. Eight species are listed as extinct or probably extinct. We will almost certainly never see these bats again. Twenty-five species are listed as endangered. They are in real danger of extinction if they cannot be protected. About two hundred other species are listed as vulnerable or potentially vulnerable. This means that they are teetering on the edge of survival. They could easily become endangered.

The most interesting thing about the list is that for almost half of the species, there is no answer. Scientists do not yet know enough about those species to decide whether they are endangered, vulnerable, or stable.

People can live comfortably near bats, and bats can live comfortably near people. The world would be a poorer place without bats. There would be many fewer flowers and flowering plants and a great many more insects. We have a great deal left to learn about these shy creatures of the night and a lot more work to do to make sure their future is secure. You can help by explaining to others how important it is to maintain healthy populations of all species of bats.

Glossary

bat detector—a scientific instrument with a microphone that can pick up ultrasonic sounds and broadcast them so that humans can hear them. A bat detector can include a tape recorder, so the bat's echolocation calls can be recorded, or it can be connected to a computer, permitting the echolocation calls to be seen as a pattern on the computer screen.

calcar—a spur on the ankle of some bats that helps support the tail membrane.

Chiroptera—the scientific order to which bats belong (see classification). Bats are sometimes called chiropterans, from the name of their order.

classification—a system used by scientists to place organisms into ever larger groups, or divide them into ever smaller groups. The basic unit is the species. From largest to smallest group, scientists use these categories: kingdom, phylum, class, order, family, genus, species. Here's a trick to help you remember the categories: King Philip came over for good sandwiches. The first letter of each word in this sentence is the same as in the classification system.

colony—a group of bats that live together. Some bats give birth and raise their young in nursery (or maternity) colonies.

diurnal—active during daylight hours.

echolocation—a system by which bats make high-frequency sounds, listen for their echoes, and use the information to navigate and locate their prey.

fossil—the remains of a plant or animal that lived millions of years ago. A fossil can be a whole organism, a small piece of it, or even a footprint or the pattern left by a leaf.

habitat—the natural environment where a plant or animal finds food and shelter

hibernate—to enter into a state of inactivity in cold weather. A hibernating mammal's breathing and heartbeat slow and its temperature drops almost as low as the air temperature where it is hibernating.

mammal—a class of animals (see classification). Mammals have hair, and female mammals produce milk to nourish their young.

mammalogist—a scientist who studies mammals

megachiropteran or megabat—an Old World fruit bat or flying fox. The order Chiroptera is divided into two suborders, Megachiroptera, the megabats, and Microchiroptera, the microbats. All the megabats are in the family Pteropodidae. Unlike microbats, their young are born with some fur, they have claws on the thumb and first finger after the thumb, and if they use echolocation, they make clicking sounds with their mouth.

microchiropteran or microbat—There are sixteen families of microbats. They all echolocate by making ultrasonic sounds with their voice boxes and listening for the returning echoes. Many microbats eat insects.

migrate—to make a seasonal movement to another location, usually from a cold place to a warmer one in the winter and back again in summer.

nocturnal—active at night.

nose leaf—a growth on the nose of some bats that seems to play a role in the direction that echolocation signals are sent.

order—When mammals are scientifically classified, they are grouped into orders. Bats are in the order Chiroptera. Humans are in the order Primates.

prey—an animal that is hunted and eaten by another animal. The animal that does the hunting is a predator.

scientific name—a two-part Latin name given to each species. Common names—the names we use—can be confusing, but scientists all over the world agree on one scientific name for each species. If you say "large slit-faced bat," you might mean a slit-faced bat that is large, but if you say *Nycteris grandis*, there is no question which bat you are talking about.

species—the basic unit into which living things (or formerly living things, like fossils or dinosaurs) are classified. Each species has a two-part scientific name.

tail membrane—a winglike, thin membrane that stretches between the legs of most bats. Scientists call this an interfemoral membrane or uropatagium.

ultrasonic—a high-frequency sound that is above the range of human hearing.

Species Checklist

Common names are confusing. More than one common name may be used for the same bat, and some common names refer to groups of bats. This list, which is alphabetical by common name, will help you find additional information about the bats mentioned in the book.

Common names are usually written in lowercase unless a proper name is part of the name. Scientific names should be italicized, with the first, or generic, name capitalized and the second name, which designates the species, in lowercase.

Australian false vampire bat (also called Australian ghost bat) *Macroderma gigas*

banana bat *Pipistrellus nanus*

big brown bat *Eptesicus fuscus*

blossom bat (also called the southern blossom bat or the common blossom bat) *Syconycteris australis*

Brazilian free-tailed bat *Tadarida brasiliensis*

California leaf-nosed bat *Macrotus californicus*

gigantic flying fox (also called the Indian flying fox) *Pteropus giganteus*

golden-tipped bat (also called Papuan trumpet-eared bat) *Kerivoula papuensis*

gray bat *Myotis grisescens*

greater bulldog bat *Noctilio leporinus*

hoary bat *Lasiurus cinereus*

hog-nosed bat *Craseonycteris thonglongyai*

Indiana bat *Myotis sodalis*

Keen's myotis *Myotis keeni*

large-eared horseshoe bat *Rhinolophus philippinensis*

large slit-faced bat *Nycteris grandis*

little brown bat *Myotis lucifugus*

long-nosed bat *Leptonycteris curasoae* (southern long-nosed bat) and *Leptonycteris nivalis* (Mexican long-nosed bat)

long-tongued bat (also called the Mexican long-tongued bat) *Choeronycteris mexicana*

painted bat *Kerivoula picta*

pallid bat *Antrozous pallidus*

red bat *Lasiurus borealis*

Seminole bat *Lasiurus seminolus*

short-tailed fruit bat (also called Seba's short-tailed bat) *Carollia perspicillata*

silver-haired bat *Lasionycteris noctivagans*

spectacled flying fox *Pteropus conspicillatus*

Underwood's mastiff bat (also called Underwood's bonneted bat) *Eumops underwoodii*

vampire bat (also called common vampire bat) *Desmodus rotundus* The other two vampire bat species are Diphylla ecaudata and Diaemus youngi.

western mastiff bat (also called western bonneted bat) *Eumops perotis*

woolly bats—22 species in the genus *Kerivoula*

yellow-winged bat *Lavia frons*

Further Research

In addition to books the authors used to write this book, the titles listed below include many featured by Bat Conservation International on their website: http://www.batcon.org/

Books for Young People

Ackerman, Diane. *Bats: Shadows in the Night*. New York: Crown Publishers, 1997.
  In this beautifully photographed book, the author retells her adventures traveling across Texas with Merlin Tuttle in search of bats.

Arnold, Caroline. *Bat*. New York: Morrow Junior Books, 1996.
  Lovely, straightforward book with wonderful photographs.

Bash, Barbara. *Shadows of Night: The Hidden World of the Little Brown Bat*. San Francisco: Sierra Club Books for Children, 1993.
  Nice illustrations; focuses on one species; some general information about bats at the end.

Graham, Gary L. *Bats of the World: 103 Species in Full Color*. New York: Golden Press, 1994.
  Good illustrations by Fiona Reid, with some photos. Tiny, straightforward book that covers 103 species grouped by families.

Jarrell, Randall. *The Bat-Poet*. New York: HarperCollins Juvenile Books, 1996.
  An eccentric little brown bat writes poems for the other forest creatures and discovers his own nature in the process.

Johnson, Sylvia A. *Bats*. Minneapolis, MN: Lerner, 1989.
  An engaging introduction to the habits of bats and the many ways bats benefit humans.

Julivert, Maria Angels. *The Fascinating World of Bats*. New York: Barrons Juveniles, 1994.
  An excellent nature book featuring scientifically accurate and bright full-color art.

Maestro, Betsy. *Bats: Night Flyers*. New York: Scholastic, 1994.
Husband-and-wife team Betsy and Giulio Maestro team up to present an excellent overview of the lives of bats from around the world.

Pringle, Laurence. *Batman: Exploring the World of Bats*. New York: Charles Scribner's Sons, 1991.
Biography of Merlin Tuttle; photos by Tuttle. Fascinating information about how he photographs bats.

Stuart, Dee. *Bats: Mysterious Flyers of the Night*. Minneapolis, MN: Carolrhoda Books, 1994.
An extensive account of bats with arresting color photographs on every page.

Web Sites

http://www.noahsays.com/animals/3.htm
Excellent summary of bat information for kids.

http://www.shop-maine.com/cov_bat/ccb_body.asp
Source for information on bat houses, including ordering information from Maine Craftsmen.

http://members.aol.com/bats4kids/
Fun site for kids, with lots of good information, games, quizzes, and excellent photos by Merlin Tuttle.

http://www.batcon.org/
Bat Conservation International - Everything you have always wanted to know about bats.

http://www.nyx.net/~jbuzbee/bat_house.html
The one-stop shopping center for bat-related sites on the World Wide Web.

Bibliography

The following books were useful and in some cases essential sources for the authors. They are useful to scientists and nonscientists alike.

Bat Conservation International. *The Vacationer's Guide to Bat Watching*.
    Austin, TX: Bat Conservation International, 1999.
    More than seventy parks, zoos, and other sites are featured in this BCI
    guide, which lists the best locations in the United States and Canada
    for viewing both captive and wild bats.

Fenton, M. Brock. *Bats*. New York: Facts On File, 1992.
    Especially good details about the behavior of bats.

Hill, John E., and James D. Smith. *Bats: A Natural History*. Austin, TX:
    University of Texas Press, 1974.
    Written for scientists, but not inaccessible.

Nowak, Ronald W. *Walker's Mammals of the World*. 6th Edition. Baltimore,
    MD: Johns Hopkins University Press, 1999.
    Includes a detailed summary of information about bats worldwide.

Richarz, Klaus, and Alfred Limbrunner. *The World of Bats*. Neptune, NJ:
    TFH Publications, 1993.
    Glossy color photos and excellent pen-and-ink drawings make this an
    attractive introduction to bats.

Strahan, Ronald, ed. *Mammals of Australia*. Washington, D.C.: Smithsonian
    Institution Press, 1996.
    Includes a species account, with one or more color photos and a
    range map, of every bat that occurs in Australia.

Tuttle, Merlin D. *America's Neighborhood Bats*. Austin, TX: University of
    Texas Press, 1988.
    Extremely useful guide to living with bats and coping with problems.

Tuttle, Merlin D., and D. L. Hensley. *The Bat House Builder's Handbook*.
    Austin, TX: Bat Conservation International, 1993.
    The definitive source for bat house information.

Wilson, Don E. *Bats in Question: The Smithsonian Answer Book.*
  Washington, D.C.: Smithsonian Institution Press, 1997.
  Everything you could ever want to know about bats worldwide.

Wilson, Don E., and Sue Ruff, eds. *The Smithsonian Book of North American
  Mammals.* Washington, D.C.: Smithsonian Institution Press, 1999.
  Includes a species account, with one or more color photos and a
  range map, of every bat that occurs in the United States and Canada.

Index

Page numbers for illustrations are in **boldface**.

temperate forest bats, 14–17
tent-making bat, **37**, 38
tragus, 61
traps. *See* captivity
tree line, 17
tropical bats, 12–14, 31–33, 35
tube-nosed bats, 39

ultrasonic, 58, 59, 94

vampire bats, 8–10, **9**, 19–20, 38, 54, 68. *see also* false vampire bats
vertebrates, 31
vespertilionid bats, 39

vision, 20, 46, 48, 61, 68
Web sites, 100
woolly bats, 84–86

yellow-winged bats, **18**, 19, 34, 80
young bats, 64–65, 72–74, **73**, **75**, 78–80, **79**

About the Authors

SUE RUFF is a freelance researcher, writer, and editor who has worked for the National Geographic Society and the Smithsonian's National Zoological Park and National Museum of Natural History. DON E. WILSON is a senior scientist at the Smithsonian's National Museum of Natural History and the author or editor of more than 160 scientific publications, including *Mammal Species of the World* (1993) and *Bats in Question* (1997), both published by Smithsonian Institution Press. They jointly edited *The Smithsonian Book of North American Mammals*, also published by the Smithsonian Institution Press.